CLASSROOM
HOW-TO

IMPROVING
STUDY HABITS

VALERIE BODDEN | ILLUSTRATIONS BY NATE WILLIAMS

CREATIVE ✶ EDUCATION

Published by Creative Education
P.O. Box 227, Mankato, Minnesota 56002
Creative Education is an imprint of The Creative Company
www.thecreativecompany.us

Design and production by Liddy Walseth
Art direction by Rita Marshall
Printed in the United States of America

Illustrations by Nate Williams © 2014

Library of Congress Cataloging-in-Publication Data
Bodden, Valerie.
Improving study habits / Valerie Bodden.
p. cm. — (Classroom how-to)
Includes bibliographical references and index.
Summary: An approachable guide to help master and apply the
writing, speaking, and listening skills involved in such habits as
setting priorities, remembering materials, and time management.
ISBN 978-1-60818-281-7
1. Study skills. I. Title.
LB1049.B573 2014
371.30281—dc23   2013029620

CCSS: RI.5.1, 2, 3, 7, 8, 9; RH.6-8.1, 6, 9; W.5.1, 2, 3, 4, 5, 7, 8, 9, 10;
W.6.1, 2, 4, 7, 8, 9; SL.6.1, 3, 4, 6

First Edition
2 4 6 8 9 7 5 3 1

TABLE OF CONTENTS

HOMEWORK. *Tests.* Speeches. **Papers.**

Does it sometimes feel like you face an endless list of tasks to complete for

school? And why? To make your teachers happy? Well, yes, completing your

work is likely to make your teachers happy. But that is not the only reason

teachers assign work. Believe it or not, writing papers, taking tests, and mak-

ing speeches benefits you, too. Every time you complete one of these tasks,

you learn something more about how to do it, and you become more pre-

pared to do it again in the future—in high school, college, and even possibly

your career. But more than that, these tasks teach you how to learn, how to

study, how to find information, and how to present your viewpoint. And such

skills will help you not only in the classroom but also in life.

Study habits, for example, teach you how to set **priorities**, how to manage your time, how to recognize important information, and how to remember facts and ideas. And those are skills that can be employed throughout your entire life, from keeping track of your schedule for babysitting jobs, sports practices, and friends' birthday parties to figuring out the important points in your mom's lecture about why you should keep your room clean. But what are good study habits? When do you need to use them? And how do you get them? Learning the answers to these questions will help you become the kind of organized, prepared student that makes any teacher happy— and it will teach you something in the process!

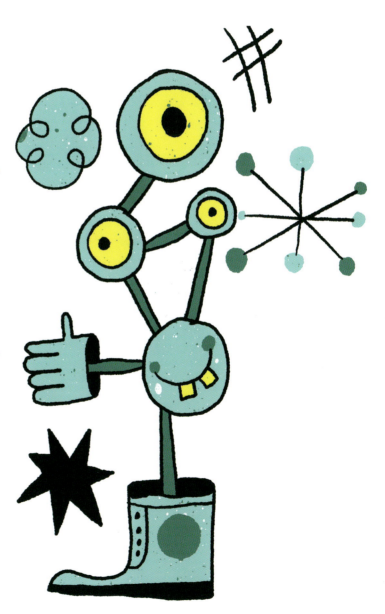

CHAPTER
ONE

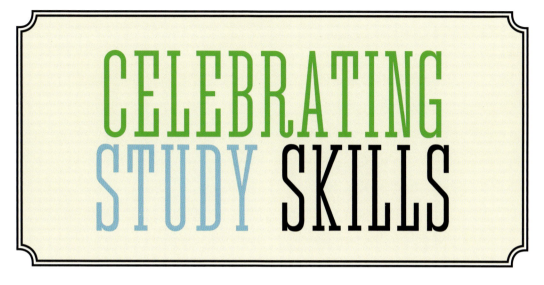

CELEBRATING STUDY SKILLS

When you think of study habits, you might think of pulling out your notebook the night before a test and skimming over all the notes you've taken in the last few weeks. Well, reviewing notes (ideally, sooner than the night before a test) is certainly a part of studying. But study habits actually encompass two separate but related ideas: learning new information comes first, and remembering that information comes second. After all, if you've never really learned a concept (not just read about it or heard about it, but really *understood* it) in the first place, how

can you expect to remember it?

Ultimately, when you learn good study habits, you are learning how to learn. And the sooner you do that, the better, because there will never be a time in your life when you can say, "I'm done" and just stop learning. Unfortunately, few schools spend time teaching study habits such as time management, prioritizing, note-taking, and creating memory tools. These skills tend to be something that you have to pick up along the way—and if you don't, you'll likely find that learning becomes more and more challenging as you progress through high school to college or other opportunities.

Of course, the immediate benefit of learning good study habits is that they can help improve your grades—and it's the rare student who would say, "No, thanks" to higher grades. Of course, your **innate** talent and abilities in a certain subject have something to do with your grades. But you'd be surprised at how much of your grade comes down to study habits. You might be a genius at algebra, for example, but unless you do the homework and study for tests, your teacher isn't likely to give you an A. Or maybe you love world history. But if you refuse to crack open your textbook or take notes, good luck passing the class. Earning better grades, in turn, can increase your self-confidence.

Although it may seem that college and a career are far away, learning good study habits now can also increase your chances of getting into college or being a successful employee. Focusing on such skills now means that when you get to high school you'll already have the skills you need to do well—hey, they'll have become regular habits by then. And your high school grades will have at least some effect on where you get into college or what job you obtain. And since these skills will be a habit, they'll benefit you in college and on the job as well. Say your first semester of college includes a science class with three textbooks and seemingly endless lectures, for example. No need to panic—just use the note-taking skills you've been practicing for years. Or what if your first job after graduation has lots of pressing deadlines? No sweat! You know how to manage your time and get everything done.

Despite its obvious advantages, learning study habits does take some

"I WOULD ADVISE YOU TO READ WITH A PEN IN YOUR HAND, AND ENTER IN A LITTLE BOOK SHORT HINTS OF WHAT YOU FIND ... FOR THIS WILL BE THE BEST METHOD OF IMPRINTING SUCH PARTICULARS IN YOUR MEMORY, WHERE THEY WILL BE READY, ... ON SOME FUTURE OCCASION."

— Benjamin Franklin

SOUNDS LIKE YOU NEED SOME HELP

work. And the first challenge is to figure out what you're already good at and what you struggle with. After all, you can't fix a problem that you don't know exists. So think about your school performance. Are you always losing assignments (or forgetting to do them in the first place)? Sounds like you need some help with organization and time management. Do you read things and then immediately forget them? Or do you find yourself frantically trying to scribble down every word your teacher says until you finally give up? Then you need to work on your note-taking skills. Maybe you're the kind of student who gets everything done and takes great notes, but you just can't remember what you've learned when it comes time for the big test. You could use some study tools and tips.

Another challenge in establishing good study habits is that not everyone learns in the same way—and yet teachers often treat students as if everyone can learn something by reading it in a book or by hearing it explained in class. The truth is that some people are visual learners. They learn best by reading words or looking at pictures or diagrams. Other people understand new information best when it is presented to them orally, as in a class lecture. They are known as **auditory** learners. Still others are

kinesthetic learners. They are hands-on people who need to work with or touch something in order to really comprehend it. What about you? How do you best learn and understand new information? Although you probably use more than one learning style, one may dominate. Once you've identified your learning style, you can use it to your advantage. If you are a visual

SET GOALS

learner, for example, you might study the solar system by reading a written description or looking at a picture of the planets. If you are an auditory learner, on the other hand, you might listen to a podcast and repeat the facts to yourself. And if you are a kinesthetic learner, you might find it most helpful to work with a model of the solar system that you can manipulate.

As you set out to learn study habits, it can also be helpful to set goals. You're not learning study skills simply for the sake of learning them. You're learning them to help you achieve

some purpose. Maybe your goal is to complete all your English assignments on time this week. Maybe it's to be prepared for next month's big social studies test. Or perhaps it's to get an A in math class this semester. No matter what your goal is, write it down. Then put it somewhere that you'll see it every day. That way, when you're feeling less than **motivated** to work on your

study habits, you'll remember why you're doing this. Oh, and be sure to promise yourself a reward when you've met your goal. So what are you waiting for? It's time to get working toward that goal—and that reward!

CHAPTER
TWO

GETTING IT TOGETHER

Maybe you have every intention of learning—and using—better study habits. But you just can't find the time to do so. Don't worry, you're not alone. Many people—students and adults alike—are haunted by the fact that there just don't seem to be enough hours in the day to get everything done. That's why time management is a huge part of learning good study habits. Before you can even sit down to study, you need to figure out how to fit it in.

And you *do* need to fit it in. Every day. "What?" you gasp. "Every day?" Yes, in order to improve your study skills, you need to make a commitment to studying every day. And that means that you need to set aside time for it. If you don't, you'll likely find that, at the end of the day, you have done everything *except* study. So, sit down with a calendar and fill out your regularly scheduled commitments— the ones that you can't break, such as school, sports practice, a babysitting job, or volunteer time. Then look at what time you have left. Also consider

"WHAT ONE KNOWS IS, IN YOUTH, OF LITTLE MOMENT; THEY KNOW ENOUGH WHO KNOW HOW TO LEARN."

— Henry Adams

when you are at your best. Are you a morning person? Do you concentrate best after a good meal? Now, block off that time (if it's available) for studying. If possible, try to schedule your study time for the same time each day. That way, when the clock rolls around to 5:00 P.M., for example, your brain will be ready to kick into study mode.

How much time do you need? That depends on how long it typically takes you to do your homework. If you're not sure, keep track of how long you spend studying for a few days. And be

In fact, studies have shown that it's beneficial to study in shorter chunks. So maybe you want to study in half-hour increments spread out through-out the day. Or you can schedule one long block of time but plan to take breaks and switch subjects every 45 minutes or so.

Once you have a *time* set aside to study, you'll need a *place* to study. While you could probably plop down anywhere (the couch, the dining room table, the family room floor) to study, certain places are more **conducive** to getting things done than others.

CHOOSE A TOPIC, & RESEARH

sure to add on time for things such as regularly reviewing your notes or reading your textbook, if you don't already do those tasks. Don't worry, though, you don't need to block out a two-hour stretch for studying. That would tax anyone's concentration!

First of all, you want to choose an area that's free of distractions. That means stay away from the TV, your little sister's yelling, and phone calls. Noise should be at a minimum. You also need somewhere well-lit and comfortable—but not so comfortable that you'll doze instead of diving into your work. A desk in your bedroom or a family office is ideal. Or maybe you find that you get your best work done at the library.

Now that you have your study time and place worked out, all you need to do is sit down and study, right? Well, yes. But have you ever found that when you do actually sit down to study it turns out that you'd rather be doing anything else? Maybe checking your e-mail or posting on a friend's Facebook page. Maybe sending a quick text. Maybe even doing the dishes. If so, your problem is **procrastination**. You want to put off until later (or never) what you know you should be doing now. The first step is to eliminate the distractions. Turn off the computer (if you won't need it for your schoolwork) or at least promise yourself that you won't check your e-mail or Facebook until your work is done. Leave the

phone in the other room. Promise your mom you'll do the dishes later (when you'll probably find that the urge to do them has gone away). If you still aren't in the "mood" to study, do it anyway. Chances are that once you get into your work, you'll feel ready (if not eager) to keep going.

Maybe your problem isn't distractions, though. Maybe you procrastinate because you think you work better under the pressure of a deadline. Paper due tomorrow and you haven't started it? No problem, you'll just pound it out tonight. Well, maybe you will. But what if something else comes up? What if your computer crashes? What if you just can't think of anything to write? It may feel like you work better under pressure, but there may come a time when that tactic doesn't hold true—and it will cost you. In the long run, procrastinating

will cause you needless stress as well, as you worry about the pressure of going from one deadline to the next.

One of the best ways to prevent procrastination is to write down your deadlines. Get a calendar or an assignment planner and—here's the key—use it. Any time a teacher gives you a deadline, write it down. Don't assume that you'll remember it (you probably won't), don't jot it on your hand (where it's likely to be washed or rubbed off), and don't scribble it inside a different notebook (where you may not notice again until it's too late). Keep track of all your assignments in your planner. Then you'll be able to see deadlines ahead of time—and you'll know when you need to start planning to meet them. That way you won't suddenly be so overwhelmed by urgent deadlines that you

BREAK IT DOWN INTO SMALLER PARTS

feel pressured, frustrated, and ready to give up.

In addition to your planner, you might want to make a to-do list of all the tasks you need to accomplish on a given day. Maybe you want to read some *Lord of the Flies* for English class, do your math homework, and start studying for Friday's science test. Great! Write it all down. And be specific. How many pages of *Lord of the Flies* do you need to read today? How much of your math homework would you like to get done? What do you need to do to start studying for science? Review your notes, make flash cards, read the text? Setting specific tasks will allow you to know when you have accomplished them— and it sure will feel good to check them off!

If you have a large task that isn't due for a few days or weeks, break it down into smaller parts. Set yourself a deadline for accomplishing each part. That way, the entire task won't seem so overwhelming and you'll get to celebrate lots of little victories along the way to completing the project. If you have to write an essay, for example, you might break it into five steps: choose a topic, research,

outline, write, and **revise**. Set aside different amounts of time for each task. Before you know it, the essay will be ready to turn in—and it may just be the best you've ever written!

You don't simply have to start at the top of your to-do list and work your way to the bottom, though. After making your list, you'll want to prioritize the items on it. Which things do you absolutely have to get done today? And which count for the largest portions of your grade? Make them top priority. Then fit the other tasks in, in order of importance or in order of deadline. You'll probably want to do your highest-priority items first, just to make sure they get done. But if you have several items of equal priority, you get to decide which to do first. Maybe you want to do all the easy assignments first so that you can spend the rest of your time concentrating on the more difficult work. Or maybe you'd rather get the hard stuff out of the way so that you can breeze through the easier assignments when you start to get fatigued. Perhaps you like to move back and forth between projects, spending a while on one, then setting it aside to work on something else before returning to the first project. Use whatever method works best for you.

Finally, whenever you sit down

to study, do so with the intention of giving your work your full concentration. This may take some practice at first, especially if you want to study for longer periods of time. When you feel your mind beginning to wander, force yourself to work another five minutes before taking a break. Soon you'll find that you can sit and think about your biology notes for 45 minutes straight. Remember, if you're going to sit down to study, you might as well do your best work. After all, if you don't do it right the first time, you may have to do it again later—and that's just a waste of time. Besides, your best work will earn your best grade. So set your study time, your study place, and your to-do list—and then get to work!

YOU MAY HAVE TO DO IT AGAIN

CHAPTER
THREE

WRITING IT DOWN

No matter how good your memory is, you cannot possibly remember every important point your teacher makes in class or every new concept covered in your textbook. That's what notes are for. And while you may find note-taking boring, confusing, or just plain painful (hand cramp, anyone?), the good news is that taking notes the right way can help you learn the material faster. Anytime you *do* something with information you've been given—rather than letting it pass in one ear and out the other—you're giving your brain one more chance to think about and remember it.

So, let's start with classroom lec-tures. Should you just write down everything your teacher says? Good luck. Even if you could manage to record your teacher's words **verbatim**, doing so would benefit you little come test time because you wouldn't know which ideas were the most important. At the same time, you do need to write down enough information to ensure that you'll understand your notes when you review them later. The goal in note-taking is to figure out which points are important and then write those down.

But how do you figure that out? If you're lucky, your teacher will say something like, "This is important," or "You'll need to know this for the test."

But if not, he'll still give you clues. If he writes something on the board or shows it on PowerPoint, for example, write it down—it's important. If he pauses dramatically, slows his speech, or repeats himself, the information he's giving then is likely important, too. There's no need to take notes on things you already know, though. If you know, for example, that George Washington was the first president of the United States (you should), don't write that down. But if you don't know when or why or how he became president, then by all means, take notes on those facts.

So that's the *what* of taking notes. But *how* should you take notes? Over the years, students and experts have developed several different note-taking systems. You should choose the one that works best for you—or even make up your own. The simplest way to take notes is to make a dash at the beginning of each new note. You might indent sub-points or related materials under the initial line of notes. The advantage of this system is that it's quick and you don't need to worry about concentrating too hard on where to write each note; instead, you can pay attention to your teacher's next thought. The disadvantage, though, is that your information may end up rather disorganized, especially if your teacher tends to skip around a lot.

If you'd prefer more organized notes, you might decide to write them in a traditional outline format, with roman numerals (such as I, V, and X) to indicate main topics, capital letters to indicate sub-topics, and arabic numerals for related details. Creating such a strict outline works well only if your teacher presents the information in an outline format, though; otherwise, you might spend too much time trying to make the material fit into your format and not enough time listening to what your teacher is saying.

Many study skills experts recommend taking notes according to what is known as the Cornell method. First, draw a vertical line from the top to the

OR EVEN MAKE UP YOUR OWN

bottom of your paper. About one-third of the page should be to the left of the line; the rest is to the right. Then, during class, you take notes in the right-hand column. Afterward, you review your notes and write key ideas, terms, and dates in the left-hand column. The idea is that these key words will serve as "clues" to what's important as you later study for a test.

Other experts advocate using mind maps or webs. To create a mind map, place the central idea of the lecture

NOTE-TAKING

in the middle of the page and circle it. Then, draw lines from that circle to sub-points, or related ideas (circle those, too). Any further details can be drawn off the relevant sub-points. When you're done, you'll likely have something that looks a bit like a spiderweb. The web will help show relationships between ideas that you might not otherwise see with other methods of note-taking.

No matter what

system you use for taking notes, be sure to keep all notes for one class in the same place. And as you write, leave plenty of space to add information you missed when you review your notes later. You can save time if you also adopt your own **shorthand**. You can use common abbreviations, such as "w/" for "with" or "b/c" for "because." And you can even invent your own shortcuts. For English class, you might use "para" for "paragraph," for example, or "WS" for "William Shake-

speare." Just be sure that you'll recognize your abbreviations when you read your notes later. You can make a key to those abbreviations at the front of your notebook. But don't use so many abbreviations that you have to look them up as you take notes—otherwise your note-taking will prove to be more time-consuming rather than less.

All your hard work taking good notes will do you little good, though, if you write them down and then never look at them again. As soon after class as possible (immediately, if you can), you should take a quick glance through your notes and write down anything you may have missed during the lecture. If you don't get it down now, it will soon be gone from your memory for good. It can also be helpful to review today's notes right before tomorrow's class, since your teacher is likely to pick up where he left off. And be sure to review your notes later in the week—and the next week and the next—as well. It may sound like a lot of extra work, but the more you look at your notes, the easier they will be to study and remember come test time.

Your teacher's lectures are not the only things to take notes on, however. If your class has a textbook and your teacher assigns you to read it, as most do, then you need to do so. While textbooks don't always make for exciting reading, they can help to explain con-

cepts that your teacher goes over in class and even supplement them with information that he doesn't mention—but that could appear on a test. Reading your textbook doesn't mean simply reading it, though. It means really thinking about and doing something

with what you read. And that usually means taking notes.

In some ways, taking notes from a reading assignment is easier than taking notes from your teacher's lectures. After all, your teacher doesn't have a rewind button, but you can take your time and reread when making notes on a book. Before you even begin to read and take notes on your textbook, though, spend 5 to 10 minutes previewing the chapter you've been assigned. Skim the introduction and conclusion of the chapter, chapter headings, and bold words. Look at pictures and diagrams. And if there are questions at the end of the chapter, read those. Now you will have an idea of the important points in the chapter, so you'll know what to look for when writing your notes.

As with lecture notes, don't write down everything. Instead, note key concepts, terms, and dates—and write them in your own words. Rephrasing what the author has said gives you one more chance to think about what you are reading and will help to ensure that you actually understand it. Again, the format of your notes is up to you. Outlining a chapter of text is generally easier than outlining lecture notes, since most textbooks are written according to an organized outline, but if you'd prefer to use a mind map, then by all means, do so. As with lecture notes, be sure to review your textbook notes often, including right after you finish taking them. You may even consider reading and taking notes on the

"THERE IS NO ONE WHO CAN SAY THAT THIS OR THAT IS THE BEST WAY TO KNOW THINGS, TO FEEL THINGS, TO SEE THINGS, TO REMEMBER THINGS, TO APPLY THINGS, TO CONNECT THINGS AND THAT NO OTHER WILL DO AS WELL. IN FACT, TO MAKE SUCH A CLAIM IS TO TRIVIALIZE LEARNING, TO REDUCE IT TO A MECHANICAL SKILL."

— Neil Postman

book before your teacher presents the topic and then adding new information from lectures to your reading notes. This method can give you a sneak peek at the information your teacher is going to present.

In addition to completing any assigned reading, be sure to complete all assigned homework. Even if your teacher doesn't grade homework (although she probably does), it is a great tool for helping you learn a new concept. And it's excellent preparation for future tests, since teachers often base test questions directly on homework questions. So don't just rush through your assignments—really give them your attention. And if you're having trouble with a concept, you might even consider doing additional work beyond what your teacher assigned. You may not get credit for it, but it'll help you understand what you need to know. And that's the whole idea of taking notes and doing homework—understanding the concepts being taught.

DON'T JUST RUSH THROUGH YOUR ASSIGNMENTS

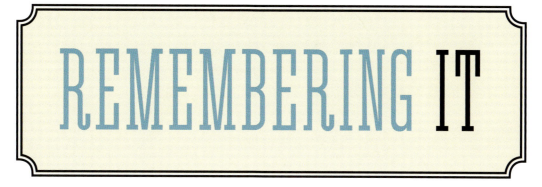

REMEMBERING IT

So you've gotten organized, set your priorities, taken your notes, and done your homework. You're really getting it together! Now, you just need to remember what you've learned. Unfortunately, sometimes that's easier said than done. Luckily for you, though, there are many tips and techniques that can help you retain, or remember, all the information you've been working so hard to learn.

In order to understand how to improve your memory, it can help to first understand a little bit about how the memory works. You don't automatically remember everything you see and hear. In fact, you forget most of it after a few minutes or a couple of hours. That's because most information never makes it past your short-term memory. You might need to remember a new friend's phone number only long enough to dial it, for example. Then you put it out of your mind—and out of memory. A person's short-term memory can generally hold only about seven items at a time. Try to put something else in, and it will likely push one of the other items out.

Long-term memory is where our brains keep the information that we need to remember for a long time. But how do we get that information into the long-term memory? Often, events that have an impact on us or that stir up powerful emotions remain in our memories. So if you've ever gotten

remember your friend's phone number forever rather than just for a few moments, you might write it down a few

REMEMBER FOR A LONG TIME

caught in a rainstorm, you might use that experience to help you remember the stages of the water cycle (one of which is precipitation). Another way to get information into your long-term memory is by doing something with it. The more we interact with information, the better the chances are that we'll remember it. So if you want to

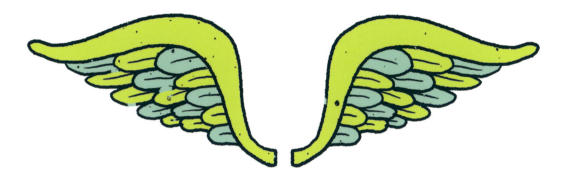

times, repeat it to yourself over and over again, or dial it every day. Soon it will be stuck in your head.

The first key to really *remembering* information long-term is *understanding* it. For example, you can memorize Newton's first law of motion: An object at rest stays at rest and an object in motion stays in motion with the same speed and in the same direction unless something pushes or pulls on it. But if you don't know what that means, then the definition is simply a bunch of words to you rather than a meaningful concept. And it's much harder to re-member meaningless words. So if you're having trouble understanding any of the concepts from your class lectures, reading, or homework, be sure to get help sooner rather than later.

That said, it is possible to memorize facts by **rote**. The problem with rote memorization is that as soon as you complete the task you were memorizing for, you may forget everything you've

spent so much time memorizing. Instead of memorizing by rote, it's usually best to commit the information you need to know to your long-term memory. And remember, the more you do with the information, the better you're likely to remember it. So choose your favorite memory techniques and use them in combination.

One of the first secrets to remem-bering information long-term is to create associations, or connections, between the information you want to remember and things you already know. Or you can make associations between several items you are trying to remem-ber. One way to do this is by grouping items into lists. In general, keep each list to seven or fewer items and try to group like items together. If you need to learn state capitals, for example, you might group all the states that begin with "A" together. Or, if you like to think geographically, you might group all the northeastern states together, and so on.

Visualization is another way to form associations that can aid memory. The idea is simple: as you're trying to remember something, create a picture of it in your mind. If you're trying to remember the Spanish word for "cake," for example, you might picture a cake with the word *bizcocho* spelled out on top in frosting. If it helps, you could even go so far as to draw the image. That way, whenever you study, you will see the picture. And by the time you need to recall the word for cake on a test, the picture should instantly pop into your head.

Even if you're not an artist, using your pen should generally be a major part of studying. Why? Unless you have to take an oral test, you'll likely be spending your entire test time writing. So spend some time rewriting your notes beforehand. Try to organize them and make connections as you do so—simply copying them is a rather mindless activity that won't necessarily help you recall information when

"FACTS ARE TO THE MIND THE SAME AS FOOD TO THE BODY.... THE WISEST IN COUNCIL, THE ABLEST IN DEBATE, AND THE MOST AGREEABLE COMPANION IN THE COMMERCE OF HUMAN LIFE, IS THAT MAN WHO HAS ASSIMILATED TO HIS UNDERSTANDING THE GREATEST NUMBER OF FACTS."

— Edmund Burke

you need it. You might also consider doing a practice test—either one supplied by your teacher or one you've made on your own.

One of the best uses of your writing time can be to create flash cards. Although they are rather low-tech and have been around for years, flash cards continue to be an effective study tool. All you have to do is write a word or a question on one side of an index card. Write the definition of the word or the answer to the question on the other side. Then, quiz yourself. You can write out the answers to the questions (another chance to write!). You can also think the answers to yourself or—even better—say them out loud.

"But won't I feel foolish talking to myself?" you might ask. Well, you could, but it's worth it. Talking to yourself gives you a chance to engage another sense (hearing) in the learning process. So get talking. You can even make a recording of yourself reading your notes or flash cards to listen to when you have extra time. If you'd rather not talk

to yourself, discuss your material with friends or have your parents quiz you. The more you hear yourself say the information, the better the chance that you'll "hear" the answers in your head when it comes time to take a test.

You can make reciting even more effective by making up a song or a rhyme using the information you need to remember. Think about it. How many songs have you memorized without even trying? And you probably still know all the words to "Twinkle, Twinkle Little Star," even though you haven't recited it in years. Song and rhyme are incredibly effective memory tools. So use them.

Similarly, you might create a

mnemonic—or memory tool—to help you remember items in a list. Usually, a mnemonic makes a word or phrase out of the first letters of something you are trying to remember. A mnemonic for the order of the notes on the lines of a treble musical staff, for example, is "**E**very **g**ood **b**oy **d**oes **f**ine." You don't have to stick with common mnemonics, though. Have some fun making up your own. Just make sure they're not harder to remember than the facts themselves! Mnemonics can be useful for memorizing by rote, but if you need to actually explain the concepts involved, make sure you understand them first. Using a mnemonic to memorize the stages of photosynthesis, for example, will do

HAVE SOME FUN MAKING UP YOUR OWN

STUDY HABITS
WON'T HAPPEN OVERNIGHT

you little good if you don't know what happens at each stage.

If you have a dramatic flair, you might prefer to study using **role-playing**. If you're learning about the Declaration of Independence, you might pretend to be Thomas Jefferson struggling to draft the document and then presenting it to the Second Continental Congress. You might even have fun enlisting friends' help—just be sure to remain focused on understanding and remembering the material.

Whichever study tools you choose to use, remember that repetition is key. Don't just study something once and then think you're done with it. It'll soon disappear unless you study

the information again and again. Just because you've repeated something over and over again doesn't mean that it will always come easily to the forefront of your brain when you need it, though. During stressful situations such as tests, information can be harder to recall on demand. If you can't remember something right away, don't panic. Instead, think about related ideas. Remember, you've made all kinds of associations with this idea—visual, auditory, and maybe even dramatic—so it's in there somewhere. As you think of related ideas, you just might come up with the answer you're looking for.

Improving your memory and your

YOU SHOULD SMILE

study habits won't happen overnight. But that's the point. Learning study habits isn't a one-time deal; it's on-going. And, eventually, your new study habits *will* pay off, in the form of a more organized life, better grades, increased self-confidence, better understanding of course materials, an improved memory—or all of the above. Soon, you'll be the kind of student that makes any teacher smile. And you should smile, too; after all, you've learned a new set of skills that you'll be able to make use of for the rest of your life!

GLOSSARY

auditory: having to do with the sense of hearing

conducive: tending to lead to something else or help something happen

innate: in-born; a skill or ability that a person is born with rather than learns through experience

kinesthetic: having to do with body position and movement

motivated: determined or having a reason to do something

priorities: items thought of as being more important than others

procrastination: the act of putting off doing something until a later time

revise: to rewrite for the purpose of improving

role-playing: the acting out of a part

rote: repetition of something, with little further thought or understanding

shorthand: a method of writing quickly by using letters, symbols, or abbreviations to stand for full words or phrases

verbatim: word for word

visualization: the act of picturing something in the mind

SELECTED BIBLIOGRAPHY

Crossman, Anne. *Study Smart, Study Less: Earn Better Grades and Higher Test Scores, Learn Study Habits That Get Fast Results, Discover Your Study Persona.* Berkeley, Calif.: Ten Speed Press, 2011.

Ellis, Dave. *Becoming a Master Student.* 14th ed. Belmont, Calif.: Cengage Learning, 2

Fry, Ron. *Get Organized.* 3rd ed. Clifton Park, N.Y.: Thomson Delmar Learning, 2005.

——. *How to Study.* 7th ed. Boston: Cengage Learning, 2012.

Hansen, Randall S., and Katharine Hansen. *The Complete Idiot's Guide to Study Skills.* New York: Alpha, 2008.

Kesselman-Turkel, Judi, and Franklynn Peterson. *Study Smarts: How to Learn More in Less Time.* Madison: University of Wisconsin Press, 2003.

Paul, Kevin. *Study Smarter, Not Harder.* 3rd ed. North Vancouver, B.C.: Self-Counsel Press, 2009.

The Princeton Review. *The Anxious Test-Taker's Guide to Cracking Any Test.* New York: Random House, 2009.

READ MORE

Book Builders LLC. *How to Study for Success*. Hoboken, N.J.: J. Wiley & Sons, 2004.

Carter, Jarrett G., Janae J. Carter, and Jolene T. Carter. *A Kid's Guide to Organizing*. Uniondale, N.Y.: Jehonadah Communications, 2002.

James, Elizabeth, and Carol Barkin. *How to Be School Smart: Super Study Skills*. New York: Lothrop, Lee & Shepard Books, 1998.

Schumm, Jeanne Shay. *School Power: Study Skill Strategies for Succeeding in School*. Minneapolis: Free Spirit, 2001.

WEBSITES

DVC Learning Style Survey for College
http://www.metamath.com/multiple/multiple_choice_questions.html
Answer a short questionnaire to discover your learning style and get information about that learning style.

How-to-Study.com
http://www.how-to-study.com/
Find study, note-taking, and memory tips.

Study Skills for Middle School
http://www.fmschools.org/eagle-hill.cfm?subpage=1328
Find study tips and ideas specifically for middle school students.

Note: Every effort has been made to ensure that the websites listed above are suitable for children, that they have educational value, and that they contain no inappropriate material. However, because of the nature of the Internet, it is impossible to guarantee that these sites will remain active indefinitely or that their contents will not be altered.

INDEX